Gulnur Amirkhankyzy

Kazakhstan's International Economic Relations

Gulnur Amirkhankyzy

Kazakhstan's International Economic Relations

Problems and prospects of development of international economic relations of the Republic of Kazakhstan

ScienciaScripts

Imprint

Any brand names and product names mentioned in this book are subject to trademark, brand or patent protection and are trademarks or registered trademarks of their respective holders. The use of brand names, product names, common names, trade names, product descriptions etc. even without a particular marking in this work is in no way to be construed to mean that such names may be regarded as unrestricted in respect of trademark and brand protection legislation and could thus be used by anyone.

Cover image: www.ingimage.com

This book is a translation from the original published under ISBN 978-3-8443-5007-4.

Publisher:
Sciencia Scripts
is a trademark of
Dodo Books Indian Ocean Ltd., member of the OmniScriptum S.R.L Publishing group
str. A.Russo 15, of. 61, Chisinau-2068, Republic of Moldova Europe
Printed at: see last page
ISBN: 978-620-3-04347-1

Copyright © Gulnur Amirkhankyzy
Copyright © 2021 Dodo Books Indian Ocean Ltd., member of the OmniScriptum S.R.L Publishing group

Introduction

International relations are a set of economic, political, legal, ideological, diplomatic, military, cultural and other ties and relations between subjects acting on the world stage.

The main feature of international relations is the absence of a single, central core of power and governance. They are built on the principle of polycentrism. Therefore, natural processes and subjective factors play a major role in international relations. International relations act as a space where different forces - state, military, economic, political, social and intellectual - collide and interact at different levels of global, regional, multilateral and bilateral.

International relations between states are one of the foundations on which modern society is built. Today, the very existence of civilization depends on relations between states.

Modern international relations are a complex system of political, economic, cultural and other relations. To date, there are several global trends in international relations. On the one hand, it is integration, creation of new international organizations and unions, on the other hand, the processes of disintegration are becoming more and more evident, and the world is becoming more polar.

An important aspect of international cooperation is economic relations between countries. Such processes as trade, international credit, labor migration, currency relations, as well as cooperation in the scientific and technological sphere can be referred to the international economic relations.

There is also quite close international cooperation between countries in science, culture and education. A variety of international exhibitions, scientific consiliums and meetings, as well as mutual exchange of students between higher education institutions of different countries, all this allows to summarize the accumulated potential of each country separately. Special mention should be made of the international space program, the implementation of which is one of the priority tasks facing the world scientific community today. Within the framework of the international space program, international studies are conducted and an international space station is functioning.

One of the most important components of international relations in the world community is international law. This concept can be characterized as a coordinated will of states, reflected in the adoption of international articles, acts and other documents regulating the relations of these states. It should be noted that there are agreements not only on interaction of states within the framework of cooperation, but also in case of conflicts of various kinds.

Today, more and more representatives of different states speak about the need to unite the world community. Many analysts have expressed their fears about the emerging trends of tension between representatives of different faiths, nationalities and races. It is the preservation of peace and tranquility on the planet, as well as the establishment of constructive cooperation that is the number one task facing today both the representatives of international organizations and representatives of individual states. [1]

Relevance of this theme is that at all times the theme of preserving the peace and security of mankind has been and will be relevant. Interaction of states, joining forces to promote economic and social progress of all peoples.

Purpose of work: to give recommendations on improving international economic relations of Kazakhstan.

The set goal is to determine the necessity of solving the following tasks:

1 . study the works of Nobel laureates in the field of international economic relations;

2 . perform an analysis of legal regulation of international economic relations;

- 3. to make recommendations and proposals on improving international economic relations in the Republic of Kazakhstan.

Acquaintance with Kazakhstan

General information

The date of independence is December **16,** 1991.

Official languages:

Kazakh - state,

Russian - official

The **capital is** Astana (653.8 thousand people).

Form of government:

Presidential-Parliamentary Republic

Territory - 2 724 900 km2

Population - 15.82 million people.

Density - 5.8 persons/km2

Time zones -UTC +5, +6.

Economic indicators

GDP

In total - $ 132.5 million.

Per capita (2008) - $ 8, 45 thousand.

Inflation rate (2008): 9.5%

The cost of consumer basket - $101

Average monthly income per capita - $ 505

Investments in fixed capital-3 836.1 billion tenge

Currency - Kazakhstan tenge (KZT, code 82)

1. 1. International organizations

Today, there is an objective trend of expansion of international relations participants. International organizations are becoming more and more important subjects in international relations. They are usually divided into interstate or intergovernmental and non-governmental organizations.

Interstate organizations are stable associations of states based on treaties, have certain agreed competence and permanent bodies. The complexity of interstate relations in the political sphere, the need to regulate international life led to the establishment of non-governmental organizations. Non-governmental organizations have a more complex structure than interstate organizations. They can be purely non-governmental, or they can be of mixed nature, i.e., they include governmental structures, public organizations and even individual members. [3]

As subjects of international relations, international organizations may enter into interstate relations on their own behalf and at the same time on behalf of all states that are members of them. The number of international organizations is constantly growing. International organizations cover a variety of aspects of international relations. They are created in the economic, political, cultural and national spheres, have certain features and specifics. Examples of various international organizations are: regional organizations such as the Association of Southeast Asian Nations (ASEAN), the European Economic Community (EEC, Common Market), the League of Arab States (LAS), economic organizations covering the field of finance, trade and so on.

Further, for example: International Chamber of Commerce (ICC), International Monetary Fund (IMF), organizations in selected sectors of the world economy, for example: International Energy Agency (IEA), International Atomic Energy Agency (IAEA), Organization of the Petroleum Exporting Countries (OPEC), political and economic organizations, for example: Organization of African Unity (OAU), professional organizations: International Organization of Journalists (IOJ); International Criminal Police Organization (INTERPOL), demographic organizations:

Democratic Women's Federation (DWFW), World Youth Association (WYM), cultural and sports organizations: International Olympic Committee (IOC), United Nations Educational, Scientific and Cultural Organization (UNESCO), military organizations: North Atlantic Treaty Organization (NATO), Pacific Security Pact (PSCAP), trade union organizations: International Trade Union Confederation (ITUC), World Confederation of Labour (WCL), various peace and solidarity organizations: World Peace Council (WPC), religious organizations: World Council of Churches (WCC), Christian Peace Conference . [1]

The most significant role in the system of international relations is played by the United Nations (UN). It has become practically the first mechanism in the history of wide multi-faceted interaction of different states in order to maintain peace and security, promote economic and social progress of all peoples. Established in 1945, the UN has become an integral part of the international structure. Its members are 192 states, which indicates that it has achieved almost complete universality. No major event in the world has been left out of the sight of the United Nations.

A number of organizations have formed within the framework of the UN, which organically entered into the system of international relations both as UN structures and as independent organizations. These include:

WHO (World Health Organization);

ILO (International Labour Organization);

IMF (International Monetary Fund);

UNESCO (Culture and Science Organization);

IAEA (International Atomic Energy Organization);

UNCTAD (UN Conference on Trade and Development);

International Court of Justice.

One of the UN departments is UNESCO (United Nations Educational, Scientific and Cultural Organization). The main purpose of this organization is to strengthen peace and security by establishing cooperation and integration ties between different states.

UNESCO supports and promotes international cooperation in various fields, in particular education, science, culture to ensure respect among nations, peoples and races, justice, the rule of law and human rights and fundamental freedoms as enshrined in the UN Charter for all peoples, without distinction as to race, sex, language or religion [1].

Kazakhstan and the UN
Tasks:

1. Preserving world peace
2. Creating a framework for sustainable development and harmonization of attitudes

   between members of the world community
3. Establishment of a fair and world order in politics and economics
4. Work to ensure the strategic interests of Kazakhstan in the international arena in the field of verbal and regional security.

Objectives:

1. Maintain international peace and security

2. To develop friendly relations between nations

3. Carry out cooperation in solving international problems and promoting respect for human rights

4. To be a center for coordinating the actions of the nation in achieving common goals.

Kazakhstan and the EU

1. State program "Way to Europe" for 2009-2011, (adopted by presidential decree

in August 2008).

2. European Union Strategy for Central Asia 2007-2013, (adopted by the EU Council in Brussels in June 2007).

Agreements:

1. Peaceful use of nuclear energy.

2. Partnership and cooperation in nuclear fusion and thermonuclear power.

3. Cooperation in nuclear safety.

Kazakhstan and the OSCE

January 1992 - Kazakhstan became a member of the Organization.

Kazakhstan elected as OSCE Chairman for 2010

Objective: to develop strategic guidelines in the light of new challenges and threats and to transform into an effective international organization adequate to the realities.

SCO (Shanghai Cooperation Organization) 2001.

Aims: strengthening of mutual trust, friendship and good neighborhood; promotion of effective cooperation in political, trade and economic, scientific and technical, cultural, educational, energy, transport, environmental and other spheres.

CIS 1991. (Commonwealth of Independent States)

UNESCO 1992. (Cultural and Scientific Organization) OIC 1995. (Organization of Islamic Countries and Kazakhstan)

2. Kazakhstan's International Economic Relations

At present, Kazakhstan's export potential has a pronounced raw material orientation and is formed by the fuel, metallurgical and chemical complex. In the structure of Kazakhstan's export the main share is occupied by oil and oil products, other important commodity groups are non-ferrous metals, ferrous metals, ores, a certain part of export falls on grain crops.

The main imported products are machinery and equipment, means of transport, devices and automatic machines, chemical products, mineral fuels, food products, finished goods and consumer goods.

The structure of Kazakhstani export-import from year to year is changing towards diversification of business relations. However, the share of trade with traditional partners - CIS and Baltic countries - is still large: they account for about 59% of exports and up to 63% of imports. At the same time, Russia remains the main trading partner. Trade relations with Germany, Turkey, Switzerland, Czech Republic, Italy, China, USA, Great Britain, South Korea, etc. are successfully developing from non-CIS countries. [3].

Kazakhstan is an active participant of integration processes in CIS. The Customs Union with Russia and Belarus, which came into force on January 1, 2010, is a breakthrough of all Kazakhstani integration initiatives.

The next stage of integration of the three countries will be the formation of the Common Economic Space from January 1, 2012. This is a higher level of integration, when the free movement of capital and workers will be ensured   .

Supporting regional economic associations in the CIS, the Government should intensify the processes of accession to the World Trade Organization on conditions that meet the priorities of economic development of Kazakhstan. [7]

2.1 Russian-Kazakh relations

Diplomatic relations between the Russian Federation and the Republic of

Kazakhstan were established on October 22, 1992.

Basic Russian-Kazakh documents:

Treaty on Friendship, Cooperation and Mutual Assistance of May 25, 1992.

Declaration of eternal friendship and alliance oriented in the XXI century, dated July 6, 1998.

Russia and Kazakhstan have established visa-free regime.

In 2004, the Year of Russia in Kazakhstan was celebrated (2003 was celebrated as the Year of Kazakhstan in Russia).

Based on the Agreement of the Program of Economic Cooperation for 2008-2011 dated October 4, 2007, bilateral cooperation with Kazakhstan in the economic sphere is being developed.

Embassies

There is a representative office of the Russian Federation in Kazakhstan:

Astana (Embassy)

Alma-Ata (Consulate General)

Uralsk (Consulate)

There is a representative office of Kazakhstan in the Russian Federation:

Moscow (Embassy of Kazakhstan)

Saint Petersburg (Consulate General)

Omsk (Consulate)

Astrakhan (Consulate)

Baikonur

In 1994, the cosmodrome with the city of Leninsk (now Baikonur) was leased to Russia. It is leased by Russia until 2050. The Kazakhstan party reserves the right to terminate the lease of the complex at any time at its discretion, informing the Russian party a year before the decision to terminate the lease of the complex.

Eurasia Channel.

In 2007, the Kazakh side proposed that Russia consider the possibility of creating a direct water transport connection between the Caspian Sea and the Azov-Black Sea basin, passing through Russian territory - the so-called Eurasia Canal. In case the project is implemented, Kazakhstan may get direct access to international maritime communications with the help of Russia and become a maritime power. [1]

2.2 Problems and prospects of development of trade and economic relations of Kazakhstan with Russia and China

Problems and prospects of development of trade and economic relations of Kazakhstan with Russia and China acquire urgency in the conditions of reforming the Kazakhstani economy and globalization of the world economy, which dictate the growing interdependence and interaction of national economies. Theoretical analysis of the current state of foreign economic relations of Kazakhstan with the main trade and economic partners is, in our view, the fundamental basis for the formation of national foreign economic doctrine. The nature of the new system of global and regional world order emerging today is especially evident in the Caspian-Central Asian region, which has recently become important and dynamic from the geopolitical and economic point of view. The geopolitical situation around this region, which includes Kazakhstan, Russia and China, is characterized by a combination and collision of national interests of the main centers of the world economy and politics, namely the United States, EU, Japan, Russia and China. Over the past decade and a half or two decades, the Asia-Pacific Region (APR) has attracted much attention as a zone of dynamic economic growth. It is the advance of other countries in terms of growth rates combined with a rapid increase in international competitiveness of the group of developing countries in the Asia-Pacific region that gives grounds to speak about the approaching "Pacific era", or the period when the region will become one of the centers of world economic development.

Strategies based on the outlined guidelines allowed them to successfully restructure the economy and, first of all, by choosing a model of foreign economic relations. The formation of the foreign economic doctrine of the nation-state, especially for countries moving from a planned economy to a market, predetermined that in the course of economic experiments they consolidated only structural policy. However, insufficient attention was paid to one of the most important aspects of successful functioning - the foreign economic sector of the country, which requires bringing its strategic goals into line with current tasks. This may be a consequence of forming the model of the country's development on the basis of objective analysis of conditions and initial prerequisites, taking into account the existing trends in the world economy development. According to the new foreign policy concept, the most important partners of Kazakhstan are, first of all, its nearest neighbors: Russia, Central Asian countries, China and CIS countries. The United States and the European Union occupy an independent place among the important strategic partners.

Special importance is also attached to cooperation with influential Asian countries: Japan, Republic of Korea, India, Turkey and Iran. In the process of formation of market economy, economic ties of Kazakhstan with Russia are of great importance. The Republic holds the third place in the level of foreign trade turnover between Russia and CIS countries after Ukraine and Belarus. At the same time, the growth rate of Russia's foreign trade turnover with Kazakhstan continues to grow.

At the level of foreign economic initiatives, it is worth noting the initiative of President Nazarbayev to create a new political and economic group - the Eurasian Union, which includes Kazakhstan and Russia as its most important members.

Kazakhstan has a constructive approach to all issues on the agenda of the Shanghai Cooperation Organization (SCO). The SCO was created on the principle of having a common border between China and the post-Soviet states. Kazakhstan was actively involved in preparing a document unique in the history of modern international relations, which was signed in April 1996 in Shanghai. It was an agreement on strengthening confidence-building measures in the border area. And exactly one year later, with Kazakhstan's most active participation, another agreement was signed in Moscow on the reduction of armed forces near the border and their withdrawal for 100 kilometers from the common border. Then, as a result of the positive evolution of the SCO, such components as trade and economic cooperation and cooperation in combating terrorism emerged. [4]

3. Economy of Kazakhstan in the new system of coordinates of international

In terms of economic development and the scale of economic reforms, Kazakhstan is one of the most successfully developing countries among the former Soviet republics.

The main part of production enterprises was denationalized and privatized in the country, and an economic and legal basis for a favorable economic climate was created. In comparison with other countries (except for Baltic countries) Kazakhstan takes the first place in the volume of attraction of foreign investments per capita by republics. In recent years, there has been a steady growth in the main macroeconomic indicators.

Economic transformations in Kazakhstan started back in the years of the USSR existence, in the second half of the 80s, when all-Union and republican governments adopted programs of transition to market economy. However, the mechanisms of these programs were largely taken from the arsenal of the administrative and command system and represented an attempt to introduce market elements into the existing dominant economic system.

Non-Ferrous Metallurgy

The share of non-ferrous metallurgy in the total industrial output exceeds 12%. Extracted ores are used to produce copper, lead, zinc, titanium, magnesium, rare and rare-earth metals, rolled products based on copper, lead, etc. Kazakhstan is among the world's largest producers and exporters of refined copper in terms of production level. The Republic's share in world copper production is 2.3%. At the same time, almost all copper produced in the country is exported abroad.

The main importers of Kazakh copper are Italy, Germany and other countries. Kazakhstan is the third among the newly independent states, the producer of gold, whose output and production increases every year. Over 170 gold-bearing deposits are registered in the country.

Ferrous metallurgy.

Kazakhstan occupies the eighth place in the world by iron ore reserves. Its share in world reserves is 6%. Apart from significant reserves, another advantage of Kazakhstani iron ore is its rather high quality. Of the 8.7 billion tonnes of iron ore, 73.3% are easily mined. Over 70% of iron ore mined in the country is exported. The share of ferrous metal ores, including chrome and manganese ores, in the country's total exports in 1999 was about 4%. Kazakhstan's ferrous metallurgy produces more than 12.5% of the country's industrial output. The flagship of the republic's industry is the Karaganda Metallurgical Plant Ispat-Karmet. The company has a full metallurgical cycle and specializes in the production of various types of rolled ferrous metals - sheet metal, bars, white sheet metal, pipes, etc. Metal of this plant is exported to the mills of CIS and far abroad. There are large reserves of chromite ores in Kazakhstan, on the basis of which ferroalloy plants of the republic work.

Chemical, petroleum refining and petrochemical industry. The range of enterprises of chemical and petrochemical industry of the republic includes plastics, chemical fibers and yarns, tires for cars and agricultural machinery, a wide range of rubber products, chrome compounds, calcium carbide, caustic soda and other products. There are three oil refineries producing motor gasoline, diesel, boiler fuel, aviation kerosene, oil bitumen and other petroleum products. A major phosphate ore processing facility produces yellow phosphorous (over 90% of total production in the former USSR), mineral fertilisers and synthetic detergents. The outlook for this industry is linked to the complex processing of Western Kazakhstan's oil and organising new products based on phosphate deposits.

Machine-building complex

Production of the machine-building complex in the total industrial output of the republic is about 8%. Machine-building enterprises of the Republic produce: forging and press equipment (Shymkent city), metal cutting machines (Almaty city), accumulators (Taldykorgan city), centrifugal pumps (Astana city), X-ray equipment (Aktobe city) etc. Nowadays, foreign investments are attracted to the development of mechanical engineering for organization of new productions in the republic, including medical equipment, agricultural machinery, diesel engines, equipment for food industry, electric motors and other products of industrial and technical purpose. [5]

3.1 Kazakhstan and CIS

The Commonwealth was established in accordance with the Agreement of the Republic of Belarus, the Russian Federation and Ukraine dated December 8, 1991. (Minsk). On December 21, 1991 in Alma-Ata the Protocol to this Agreement was signed, which fixed the participation in CIS of Azerbaijan Republic, Republic of Armenia, Republic of Kazakhstan, Kyrgyz Republic, Republic of Moldova, Republic of Tajikistan, Republic of Uzbekistan and Turkmenistan. In December 1993 Georgia acceded to it.

In September 1993, the Treaty on the Establishment of the Economic Union was signed. The implementation of the measures provided for by it is the main content of the modern integration stage of the Commonwealth of Independent States development.

Integration processes in the CIS are developing simultaneously at three levels: at the CIS-wide (Economic Union), at the sub-regional level (Customs Union of Belarus, Kazakhstan, Kyrgyzstan, Tajikistan and Russia, Central Asian Union) and through the system of bilateral relations.

There is a whole package of multilateral agreements between the CIS countries, which includes: Agreements on cooperation in the field of mechanical engineering (September 24, 1993), construction (September 9, 1994), chemistry and petrochemistry (September 9, 1994), on trade turnover and industrial cooperation in the field of mechanical engineering on a mutually linked basis (December 9, 1994).); Agreement on cooperation in the field of investment activity (December 24, 1993) and on creation of common scientific and technological space (November 3, 1995);

Agreement on assistance in creation and development of production, commercial, credit and financial, insurance and mixed transnational associations (April 15, 1994).

Proceeding from all the above, we can conclude that Kazakhstan is inextricably linked with the CIS, and, in fact, the union plays a significant role in the development of the country's economy. As for relations between the Republic of Kazakhstan and Ukraine, along with the insignificant exchange of industrial raw materials from Kazakhstan for Ukrainian goods, we can note the use of opportunities for Ukrainian enterprises in cooperation with Kazakh partners on commission raw materials (in the import from Kazakhstan the share of commission raw materials has reached almost 50%). Kazakhstan is the largest consumer of transport services in Ukraine among non-European CIS countries. The signing of the long-term cooperation program, during the visit of President N. Nazarbayev to Kiev in 1999, significantly intensified the economic relations of both countries. [4]

History of the Customs Union

The **Customs Union is a** single customs territory within which there is a single customs tariff in mutual trade, customs duties and economic restrictions are not applied, except for special protective, anti-dumping and compensation measures.

1834 - creation   The *Customs Union* between Prussia and Bavaria, Württemberg and other German states.

October 6, 2007 - Presidents of Russia, Belarus and Kazakhstan signed a package of documents at the summit of the Eurasian Economic Community in Dushanbe concerning the formation of the legal framework of the *Customs Union.*

October 8, 2008 - Moscow. The State Duma has ratified the package of documents on the *Customs Union of* Russia, Kazakhstan and Belarus. Agreement on creation of a single *customs* territory and formation of the *Customs Union*

June 10, 2009 - Pascal Lamy noted that in the *history of the* WTO there was no case that it included a whole block, not individual countries.

Jan 1, 2010 - MINSK, The first stage of the *Customs Union of* Belarus, Russia and

Kazakhstan begins on January 1, 2010: the unified *customs* tariff comes into force.

www. lenta. ru/news/2009/06/12/wto/

4. Positions of Nobel laureates in the direction of international economic relations

Nobel Prize in Economics, officially the Swedish State Bank Prize for Economic Sciences in memory of Alfred Nobel - the prize established by the Bank of Sweden in memory of Alfred Nobel in 1969 and awarded for achievements in economic sciences. It is the most prestigious award in the field of economics.

At the end of 2009, 64 economists were awarded the prize. The winner of the Nobel Prize in Economics is announced on October 12. The award ceremony is held in Stockholm on December 10 every year.

The first winners of the Nobel Prize in economics were the Norwegian Ragnar Frisch, who developed the principles of building "national accounts", and the Dutch Jan Tinbergen, the author of the theory of "optimal system.

The only Soviet scientist - winner of the Nobel Prize in Economics in 1975 was Leonid Kantorovich, one of the creators of the theory of optimal planning and management of the national economy, as well as the theory of optimal use of raw materials.

Nowadays, the Nobel Prize is widely known as the highest distinction for human intellect. In addition, this award can be attributed to a small number of awards, known not only to every scientist, but also to a large number of non-specialists. In 1977, Ulin Bertil and James Meade shared the Nobel Memorial Prize in Economics "for their pioneering contribution to the theory of international trade and international capital flows. In his presentation speech, Assar Lindbeck, a member of the Swedish Royal Academy of Sciences, noted that Uhlin's work "proved that it can be a strong cornerstone for further theoretical work as well as for practical applications. And that she has also "encouraged scientists to conduct a large number of research in international economics that goes beyond strictly formalized models. In his Nobel Lecture, Ulin compared "two cases of serious international depression in countries with a predominant focus on the market economy. He also drew attention to

differences in economic factors during the Great Depression and the global recession
of the mid-70s.

Table No. 1. Positions of Nobel laureates.

№	Year	FULL NAME	Proceedings
1	1977	Gotthard Ulin	"Contribution to the theory of international trade and international capital flow".
2	1977	James Edward Meade	"A pioneering contribution to the theory of international trade of international capital flows".
3	1979	William Arthur Lewis	"Developed recommendations to improve the trade balance and ensure the development of the "third world", which has a beneficial impact on regional and global trade.
4	1980	Lawrence Klein	"Project "Link", to integrate statistical models of different countries into a single common system to improve understanding of international economic relations and forecasting of world trade.
5	2008	Martti Ahtisaari	"For the important efforts he has made on several continents over three decades to resolve international conflicts.
6	2009	Barack Obama	"For extraordinary efforts in strengthening international diplomacy and cooperation between peoples".

The table was compiled by G. Amirkhankyzy. [2]

Lewis Arthur shared the 1979 Nobel Memorial Prize in Economics with the

American economist Theodore Schultz "for pioneering research on economic development.... in the annex to the problems of developing countries". In his Nobel lecture, "The Slowing Down of the Engine of Growth," Lewis combined his theories about the nature of world trade and its history with the idea that least developed countries should no longer remain dependent on developed countries for their economic growth. By expanding regional trade, he said, they can eventually accelerate their own development, even if economic growth in developed countries slows down. He also accused developed countries of "lack of awareness" of their "mutual dependence" on both types of economies.

In foreign policy, Hull Cordell shared Wilson's idealistic views and supported the League of Nations. His economic ideas were rooted in 19th-century liberalism, he believed that economic nationalism was the main cause of wars. That's why he opposed the policy of high tariffs, pursued by Wilson. Hoover. From 1939 to 1941, Hull negotiated patiently but unsuccessfully to achieve peace between Japan and China and prevent further Japanese invasions of Indochina. During this time, H. tried to strengthen the position of the moderates in the Japanese government and weaken the militarists.

In 2008, the Nobel Peace Prize winner was the Finnish diplomat Marti Ahtisaari, who was awarded for mediating many conflicts on three continents, but is best known for his plan to resolve the conflict over Kosovo, which eventually led to the declaration of independence of the republic. His peacekeeping work is not limited to Kosovo. Ahtisaari brought to a logical conclusion a struggle that all freedom-loving mankind, led by the Soviet Union, fervently supported in its time. In particular, from 1977 to 1981, he was a UN special envoy to Namibia, where he worked to end the occupation of South Africa and declare its independence.

US President Barack Obama won the Nobel Peace Prize in 2009. The award was given to him with the wording "for his great efforts to strengthen international diplomacy and cooperation between peoples. Leader of the United States, he promised to abandon the previous unilateral foreign policy and expressed willingness to take care of the interests not only of the United States, but of all countries of the world. He also stated that he was ready to negotiate with such countries as Iran, with which the United States had not maintained diplomatic relations for thirty years. One of the most important points in his election program was the completion of the military campaign in Iraq and the withdrawal of U.S. troops from there. [2]

5. Evaluation of approaches, methods and conclusions of Nobel laureates from the point of view of their use for Kazakhstan conditions.

According to Kondratyev's cycle system, in the history of capitalist economy development from the 2nd half of the 19th century two large cycles took place: the first one - from 1850 to 1900 and the second - from 1900 to 1940. From 1945 the third big cycle - the phase of "capital starvation" - began. It follows from the theory of large cycles that ordinary economic cycles disappear, the main phase of the cycle - the economic crisis of overproduction - dissolves in the oscillations of large waves. Based on Kondratyev's theory of large cycles, a scheme of possible crisis-free development of capitalist economy was constructed. In this sense, the concept of large cycles is described as being directed against the initial Marxist provision about the inevitability of economic crises under capitalism. It became most widespread in pre-war years. After World War II, its provisions formed the basis for a whole line of research in economics and were used to forecast the development of capitalist economy.

The negative side in the works of the Nobel laureates in the field of international relations is that the works of the laureates, chosen by me, belong to the third cycle of Kondratyev's theory, which is designed for capitalist countries, the Republic of Kazakhstan does not belong to the capitalist countries, so many of the works of economists on the theory of Kondratyev is not applicable to our country.

Positive sides: Since the Republic of Kazakhstan belongs to the "third world" countries, I would like to note the work of William Arthur Lewis. He has developed recommendations for improvement of trade balance and provision of development of the "third world" countries.

The reasons for trade relations between the countries were economic and natural resources that were not evenly distributed, and the production of goods required new technologies. Therefore, Kazakhstan simply needs trade relations with other countries of the world. The works of the laureates in the sphere of international economic relations are connected with the development of foreign trade between the states.

A qualitative leap in the development of productive forces - the creation and development of a large industry - was crucial for expanding economic ties between countries. Progress in the development of productive forces, which manifested itself in the increase in the scale of production, improved transportation of goods, made it possible to expand economic, including trade, ties between countries.

6. Analysis of legal regulation in the sphere of international economic relations of the Republic of Kazakhstan

Name of documents:

1. International relations in the field of environmental protection and natural resources.

• Code of the RK - "Environmental Code of the Republic of Kazakhstan", 47 chapters, 326 articles

Code of the Republic of Kazakhstan dated January 9, 2007 N 212

• Law of the RK - "On accession of the Republic of Kazakhstan to the Convention on Environmental Impact Assessment in a Transboundary Context".

Law of the Republic of Kazakhstan dated October 21, 2000 N 86-II SAK

"On ratification of the Convention on Access to Information, Public Participation in Decision-making and Access to Justice in Environmental Matters".

Law of the Republic of Kazakhstan dated October 23, 2000 N 92-II SAK

"On accession of the Republic of Kazakhstan to the Convention on the Protection and Use of Transboundary Watercourses and International Lakes".

Law of the Republic of Kazakhstan dated October 23, 2000 N 94-II

• Agreements - "Agreement on information cooperation in the field of ecology and environmental protection".

"Agreement between the Government of the Republic of Kazakhstan and the Government of the Russian Federation on cooperation in environmental protection".

• Resolution of the Government of the RK - "On approval of the Agreement on information cooperation in the field of ecology and environmental protection".

Resolution of the Government of the Republic of Kazakhstan dated August 5, 1999 N 1104

"On conclusion of the Agreement between the Government of the Republic of Kazakhstan and the Government of the Russian Federation on cooperation in the field of environmental protection".

Resolution of the Government of the Republic of Kazakhstan dated January 29, 2004 N 102

• Conventions - "Convention on Environmental Impact Assessment in a Transboundary Context"

"Convention on the Protection and Use of Transboundary Watercourses and International Lakes"

"Stockholm Convention on Persistent Organic Pollutants". Convention, Stockholm, May 22, 2001.

2. International cooperation in the field of international public organizations and funds providing grants

-Suspension of the Government of RK - "On approval of the list of international and state organizations, foreign and Kazakh non-governmental public organizations and funds providing grants".

Resolution of the Government of the Republic of Kazakhstan dated March 20, 2009 № 376

3. International cooperation in the field of international treaties

-Law of the RK - "On international treaties of the Republic of Kazakhstan".

Law of the Republic of Kazakhstan dated May 30, 2005 N 54

-Suspension of the Government of the RK - "On application of norms of international treaties of the Republic of Kazakhstan".

Normative Resolution of the Supreme Court of the Republic of Kazakhstan dated July 10, 2008 N 1.

4. International cooperation in international commercial arbitration

-Law of the RK - "On International Commercial Arbitration", 8 chapters, 33 articles

Law of the Republic of Kazakhstan dated December 28, 2004 N 23

5.   International cooperation in the search for persons

-Codex - "Criminal Procedure Code of the Republic of Kazakhstan", 577 articles

Code of the Republic of Kazakhstan dated December 13, 1997 N 206

6.   International cooperation in the field of education "Bolashak"

• Law of RK - "On Education", 12 chapters, 68 articles

Law of the Republic of Kazakhstan dated July 27, 2007 N 319-III

• Resolution of the Government of the RK - "On the establishment of international scholarships of the President of the Republic of Kazakhstan" Bolashak "for training abroad".

Resolution of the President of the Republic of Kazakhstan dated November 5, 1993 N 1394

• Presidential Decrees - "Regulations on the Republican Commission on Training Abroad".

Presidential Decree of the Republic of Kazakhstan dated October 12, 2000 N 470

• Others - "Order on some measures to implement the international scholarship Bolashak

Order of the Minister of Education and Science of the Republic of Kazakhstan dated May 19, 2009 № 224. Registered with the Ministry of Justice of the Republic of Kazakhstan on May 29, 2009 № 5684.

7. International cooperation in the field of atmospheric air protection

-Codex RK - "Ecological Code of the Republic of Kazakhstan"

Code of the Republic of Kazakhstan dated January 9, 2007 N 212

8. International cooperation in the field of innovation actors

9. icons of the RK - "On state support of innovation activity".

Law of the Republic of Kazakhstan dated March 23, 2006 N 135

10. formation of the government of the RK - "On approval of the Agreement on formation and status of interstate innovation programs and projects in scientific and technological sphere". Resolution of the Government of the Republic of Kazakhstan dated March 3, 1999 N 196

The schedule was made by Amirkhankyzy G. on the basis of the reference and information system "Law" by the method of Doctor of Economic Sciences, G. K. Kuatbaeva.

1. Having constructed dynamics and a trend line of normative-legal acts of the Republic of Kazakhstan in the field of the international economic relations for 1990-2010, it is possible to see that the government of the republic makes integration in the legislation, peaks are 2001 and 2009. The reasons for the increase in acts in 2000-2001 are related to the Asian crisis, and in 2009 - to the global financial crisis. In 2003, Kazakhstan's preparation for accession to the WTO, there was an increase in legislative acts since 2003. In 2006, the Republic of Kazakhstan is in a state of euphoria. This leads to an increase in legal acts and during the global financial crisis - 2009 reached its peak.

2. Having built a trend line, I believe that in the sphere of international economic relations of the Republic of Kazakhstan the number of normative and legal acts will increase. As if from 1990 to 1998 everything is stable, then from 1999. starts the growth caused by the Asian crisis, 2007-2009, the increase connected with the world financial crisis. Making a forecast of the development of regulatory and legal acts, I believe that by the end of 2010.

In 2012, there will be a sharp decline as the government will work on areas that were more affected by the crisis in 2009. And in 2013-2015, the increase will be due to the implementation of anti-crisis programs.

The schedule was compiled by G. Amirkhankyzy on the basis of the reference - information system "Law" by the method of Ph.

1. The reasons of prevalence of laws of the Republic of Kazakhstan and the Code in the sphere of international economic relations is that relations with the countries should be clearly specified in the laws, they make 87% of all normative and legal acts.

2. The mechanism of regulation in the sphere of international economic relations works through a set of mechanisms that are closely interconnected with each other. Such as legislation, standardization, certification, regulation, licensing, forecasting, planning, programming and design.

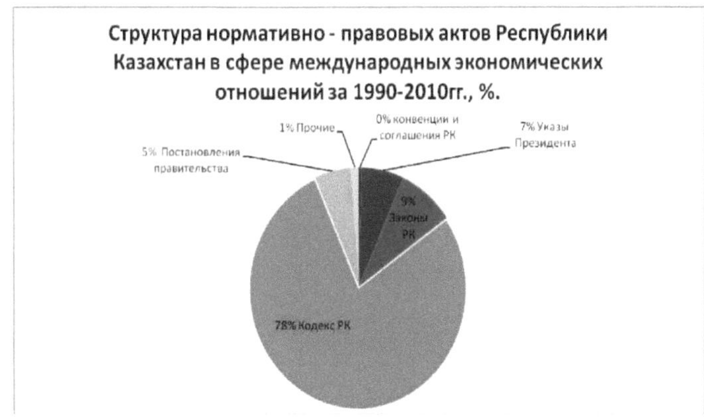

7. Strategy for the Development of International Relations until 2020.

Of particular importance is the creation of conditions for Kazakhstan's participation in the processes of global decision-making in the formation of the new architecture of international relations and the contours of the world trade and financial system. The Republic of Kazakhstan will strongly promote and vigorously defend its interests in the formation of supranational reserve currencies. The effectiveness of these efforts will largely depend on the successful implementation of Kazakhstan's anti-crisis measures, on the pace of the country's economy on the trajectory of post-crisis and sustainable development, on real achievements in the creation of innovative and diversified economy.

As an influential member of the Collective Security Treaty Organization and the Shanghai Cooperation Organization, and initiator of the Conference on Interaction and Confidence Building Measures in Asia, Kazakhstan will actively promote the establishment of a strategic dialogue between the existing systems of collective security. Kazakhstan will continue its proven policy of preventing an arms race, supporting the efforts of the international community in the field of nuclear disarmament and strengthening the Treaty on the Non-Proliferation of Nuclear Weapons regime. In doing so, it will make maximum use of the opportunities provided by Kazakhstan's chairmanship of authoritative international organizations (the Organization for Security and Cooperation in Europe, the Organization of the Islamic Conference and others).

Kazakhstan will make better use of its unique geographical position and irreplaceable role in the system of global and interregional transport communications. The country's role in ensuring global energy, environmental and food security will significantly increase. Kazakhstan will take its rightful place in the system of international division of labour and become a member of the World Trade Organization.

Kazakhstan will continue the course of strengthening the multi-speed and multi-level integration in Central Asia, in the Eurasian space. Along with Russia, Kazakhstan will form a stable core of the Commonwealth of Independent States, the Eurasian Economic Community and the Customs Union. [6]

Strategic goals in the sphere of international relations.

By 2020	
	favorable international environment is formed, friendly relations of equal cooperation with all states are maintained
	a high level of Kazakhstan's integration into the international community and world economic relations based on the diversification of the national economy was achieved
	Conditions and prerequisites for political and economic integration of the region's states are provided
	Kazakhstan is a key participant of effective system of regional security and political and economic cooperation.
	Kazakhstan is represented in governing bodies of leading international and regional financial and political structures
	Kazakhstan is an active subject of international relations and participates in making decisions that are important for world politics.

Conclusions and proposals

The Republic of Kazakhstan is a country of raw materials. On this basis, an important task is to establish foreign economic relations with other states.

Our exports include oil, natural gas, noble metals, oil refining products, copper, zinc, other nonferrous metals and their products, ferrous metals, cotton, chemical products and so on. The main share of imports falls on the purchase of equipment, clothing, footwear, furniture, food products, vehicles, chemical and pharmaceutical products. Cooperation is developing in many areas, for example, in the development of mineral deposits, processing of agricultural products, food industry, agricultural machinery, heavy and light industry, energy.

During the previous decade, Kazakhstan has laid the foundation for the future development of a country with a diversified economy, a well-educated and healthy population living in security and democracy that uses its natural resources for the benefit of all citizens. This has been greatly facilitated by increasing export revenues amid rapidly rising prices for oil and other mineral resources. The same conditions for further development of the country are not guaranteed in the next decade.

The most important lesson of the current world crisis was the understanding that the future development of the global economy is extremely uncertain and unpredictable. And this fact should be taken into account when planning the economic development of the country in the future.

The world's leading economies will operate in a more complex, competitive environment and will take preventive measures to prepare for the next economic cycle, increasing labor productivity, investing in infrastructure and telecommunications, strengthening financial systems, improving the efficiency of public administration, as well as creating favorable conditions for business development. The same tasks are strategic constants for Kazakhstan set by the "Kazakhstan - 2030" Strategy. During the next decade, Kazakhstan will work to achieve these objectives.

Kazakhstan will remain one of the largest hydrocarbon producers. At the same time, the republic will take part in solving the problem of global warming, accelerating the technological modernization of energy and development of energy saving. In order to ensure food security of the country, agriculture, especially the processing of agricultural products, will be further developed. Kazakhstan's health care system will be able to withstand new types of diseases. The efficiency of use of the country's natural resources, especially water resources, will be increased through modernization of infrastructure and formation of a policy of rational use of natural resources, taking into account the task of environmental protection.

Having a stable political environment, significant economic and human capital, rich natural resources, basic production infrastructure, sustainable financial system, Kazakhstan is able to transform the challenges created by the current global economic crisis into new opportunities to achieve balanced and sustainable development.

Taking into account the fact that implementation of large-scale plans will face tougher budget restrictions, a high level of return on public investments will be ensured and the efficiency of implementation of adopted programs will be increased. [6]

Suggestions

1. Strengthen control over the legislative framework in the sphere of international economic relations.

2. Integration and harmonization, of all types of standards and regulations to ensure quality improvements and sustainable development.

3. Searching for markets for Kazakh products, given the raw material nature of the economy, we need optimal ways to export oil.

4. Development of non-resource sector of economy

5. Attraction of investments.

Conclusion

Kazakhstan is a unique country in its own way: quite a large area, small population, a kind of tax system, historically established industry structure (predominance of production over production) and strong ties with the CIS countries.

The geography of international relations of our republic covers almost all continents. Among our partners are the leading countries of Asia, Europe, America and distant Australia. Due to balanced and multilateral policy, relations of Kazakhstan with the USA, China, Japan, France, Canada, Turkey, Iran, India, Pakistan, Egypt, Saudi Arabia, Hungary and other Eastern European countries, with the Baltic States, Scandinavia, Ukraine and Transcaucasia are successfully developing. There are signs of progress in the Latin American direction and with the states of Southeast Asia. Links with Arab world and with Muslim world in general are becoming more active.

Kazakhstan intends to participate in the processes of global decision-making in the formation of a new architecture of international relations and the contours of the world trade and financial system. Kazakhstan will actively promote the establishment of strategic dialogue between all existing systems of collective security. Kazakhstan is fully aware of its role as a responsible participant in regional and global economic processes and flawlessly performs it throughout the years of its independence. High international reputation of Kazakhstan allowed our country to become the Chairman of the Organization for Security and Cooperation in Europe. It is a great honor for us. It is the highest responsibility to chair the OSCE in the most difficult period of modern human history. OSCE with its unique geographical composition of participants - 56 states, 40.

Located on three continents, with extensive experience of interaction between states is one of the key mechanisms of international security and cooperation. Kazakhstan's chairmanship in OSCE will be aimed at development of security and prosperity of the peoples of the world. [7]

List of used literature

1. http://www.unitednations.ru/article 27.html

2. Nobel Prize Laureates: Encyclopedia: Per. engl.-M.: Progress, 1992.The H. W. Wilson Company, 1987. Added Translation into Russian, "Progress" Publishing House, 1992.

3. Nazarbayev N.A. Strategy of formation and development of Kazakhstan as a sovereign state. -1992-C. 75-93.

4. Tokaev K.K. Foreign policy of Kazakhstan in conditions of globalization. Almaty, 2000/-C/434-445

5. Khan G.B. Foreign policy of the Republic of Kazakhstan. Almaty, 2001.P.225-227.

6. Strategic Development Plan of the Republic of Kazakhstan till 2020.

7. Message from the President of the Republic of Kazakhstan to the people of Kazakhstan in 2010.

Printed by Books on Demand GmbH, Norderstedt / Germany